OMG
IT'S TRUE!

You've Always Thought
There Must Be More To This Life...

THERE IS!

AMOS ALLINGER

Focus Management Services LLC

Amos Allinger

Copyright © 2016 by Amos Allinger

Cover design: Panagiotis Lampridis

Interior Page design: Purity K

For permission contact:

FocusManagementServicesLLC@gmail.com

Library of Congress Control Number: 2016917538

ISBN: 978-0-9982468-9-5

Dedicated to:

my beautiful wife
Alexus
my beautiful children
Siara, Noah, Emyah, Avah,
Rainah, Payton, Gaberiel,
Zayden, Keelan, and Israel
my handsome grandson
Kingston
my beautiful mother
Denise
my dads
God, Rocky, and Richard
my brothers and sisters
Kristie, Les, Amy, and Rocky
and all of my awesome nieces and nephews.

CONTENTS

INTRODUCTION

At some point or another, we've all come to the same conclusion: THERE MUST BE MORE TO THIS LIFE! I'm here to bring you the good news, that you're right...THERE IS! At the turn of the new millennium, I had the privilege of stumbling upon a remarkable, life-changing Truth that I call, "God's Next Evolutionary Step for Mankind." It's a phenomenal reality, hidden in plain sight, which you can touch and feel for yourself. It's a Truth that most of us have heard of before, but have never actually experienced for ourselves.

Many people say that we are the Temple of God, that He lives inside of us, or that Jesus lives in our hearts. Well, guess what? It's true! Being the "Temple of God" is more than an idea or way of life—it's a powerful, epic discovery that awaits your asking. "God's Next Evolutionary Step for Mankind" is this: you can literally find God living inside of your heart organ and interact with Him One-on-one, all by tweaking your focus, ever so slightly, towards the heartbeat in your chest. Don't freak out, though—God has your best interests in mind and is much more loving, understanding, forgiving, and merciful, than any of us give Him credit for...and I promise that you won't burst into flames when you try this!

So, how can I confidently make this bold claim? Well, quite simply, I know that you have this unrealized potential inside yourself, because every day for the past 16 years, God has personally interacted with me inside of my heart. The first few chapters of this book contain the very raw, real, and eye-opening portrait of my crazy life, filled with many twists and turns, which you won't regret reading. By sharing my story, filled with many tragic circumstances, foolish decisions, and bizarre situations that all led me to this discovery, I believe you'll see that if God is willing to give someone like me this gift, He'll give it to you, too.

After sharing my story, I'll present some of the evidence that I've found in the Word of God to support the claim that you can find God and interact with Him inside of your heart, too. Additionally, I'll share some different exercises and methods I've used over the years so that you can have this revolutionary experience for yourself. You'll understand the depths of what this means for you and see all of the perks that come with it. This incredible gift is yours for the taking, regardless of your past mistakes or beliefs. Not only will you know that God exists and that you're His child, but you'll see that when you leave this life, you'll live forever and be reunited with your loved ones. On the other side of this difficult, confusing life, there's an unimaginable inheritance waiting for you that's beyond your wildest imagination. You'll have all the proof you'll ever need to know that this is true...in your very own body! Your life will never be the same, as you take the journey inside to discover this fascinating part of life that you likely never knew existed. It is my mission, honor, and pleasure to bring you my testimony, so please sit back and get ready to read one of the craziest life stories you may have ever heard.

CHAPTER 1:
A MIRACULOUS BEGINNING

A Baby with Purpose

It's a miracle that I even made it into this life, considering what almost happened to my mom before she was born. In early 1952, my maternal grandmother had two daughters and found out she was pregnant with a third child, my mom. She cursed God the day that she found out she was pregnant. In disappointment of being with child again, she grabbed a tree limb, peeled off the small offshoots, and attempted to perform an abortion on herself. The blood came pouring out, but luckily for my mom, siblings, and myself, my grandmother was unsuccessful, and her baby lived. Months later, in December of 1952, my mother was miraculously born into this world.

Escaping the Monsters

As my mom grew up, she continually heard her mother say that she wasn't wanted, and it was a mistake she was even here. I can only imagine how she must've felt hearing those words. However, that was nothing compared to the pain my mom experienced when she was a five-year-old girl. She recalls evenings when her parents came home from the bar with their male friends. While my grandparents were in the other room, the men would sexually assault my mom and expose themselves to her. This was only the beginning of her devastating childhood.

A few years later, my grandparents got divorced, and my grandmother remarried. For several years, when my grandmother left the house to run errands, my mom's stepdad sexually assault her, as well. My mom told her mom what was happening on multiple occasions, but instead of believing her, my grandma defended her new husband and called my mom a liar. Unfortunately, the assaults didn't stop until my mom was fifteen when she took matters into her own hands and ran away to escape this harsh reality.

Marriage, War, and Children

At this time, my mom and dad were dating. She described him as the best guy she knew at the time. He was the third oldest of eleven children, and grew up having a childhood much different than my mom's; namely, there wasn't sexual abuse of any kind in the home. After high school graduation, he joined the United States Marine Corps, to fight in the Vietnam War. After basic training, he was stationed in San Diego, California. When my mom ran away, she flew to San Diego and married my dad. My sister was born nine months later, while my dad was still in Vietnam.

While at war, my dad was exposed to the chemical "Agent Orange," which caused him to develop the mental condition schizophrenia. When he returned home from Vietnam, my mom said that he came back a different man altogether. Regardless of his condition, my mom stayed married to him and gave birth to my older brother in 1971. My parents enjoyed being part of the experimental drug culture of the 70's. My mom had decided that she was done having kids, so she started taking birth control shortly after my brother was born.

Hearing the Voice

A week before my dad had graduated from college, my paternal grandmother clipped an article from the newspaper titled, "Local Minister Claims to Hear the Voice of God." In an attempt to help my dad from destroying his life with drugs, she gave him the article. Immediately following his graduation ceremony, still dressed in his cap and gown, my dad went to the minister's office to prove that he was a liar. When he approached the minister, he held up the article and said, "So they say you can hear the voice of God. Can you prove it?" The minister asked my dad to write down any questions he wanted God to answer. My dad wrote down his questions and handed them to the minister's counterpart, a female "prophet" who claimed that she heard the audible voice of God, too. I don't know what he asked, but "God's answer" made my dad completely change his lifestyle. He gave up partying and became a devoted born-again Christian man who followed the words and teachings of these two self-proclaimed prophets. Shortly afterward, my mom followed suit, and they both became active members of the church.

During one Sunday morning church service, from the pulpit, the minister told the congregation that God said that there were women in the church who had been taking birth control and that He wanted them to stop taking it immediately. My mom felt that this message was for her, so she immediately stopped taking birth control pills, and conceived a child shortly afterward...me! When my maternal grandmother found out my mom was pregnant with her third child, she walked up to my dad, slapped him in the face, and said, "I can't believe you've gotten my daughter pregnant again and have her attending that cult of a church!" Coincidentally, just as my grandmother didn't want her third child, she didn't want my mom to have her third child either.

Strange Prophecies

A few months later, while she was five months pregnant, she went with my dad and twenty other church members to Israel for a Holy Land tour. After my parents got back to the United States from their trip, the minister said that God wanted him to write the President of the United States, Richard Nixon, something similar to the following message: "President Nixon, the voice of God has told me to tell you that He sees what you're doing, and if you don't confess to the nation what you've done, He will expose you, Himself. God says that it isn't you who pulls the strings, but Him, and warns that you are not to follow the advice of your Secretary of State because he is the Antichrist." A few days later, two Secret Service agents visited the minister's office, handed him the letter and asked, "Where did you get this information?" The minister replied, "It was God. He told me." The agents laughed at such a notion, turned around, and walked out of the church.

Around the same time, there was a missing child in the area—a boy. The minister claimed that God woke him up in the middle of the night, gave him the exact whereabouts of the boy's body, and had instructed him to give the information to the police. The police went to the location and found the corpse of the missing boy. Perhaps, like me, you question whether or not the minister had something to do with the disappearance of the child. However, only God knows the answer to that question. Interestingly enough, soon afterward, the minister ended up in the hospital with pancreatitis, and the doctor told him he may not make it and that he would likely end up dying. On his deathbed, he told his followers not to worry because he would be

6

coming back from the dead after three days and nights, like Jesus. He had died one month before I was born, but he never came back to life. It was this prophecy that led to his church splitting and eventually closing for good. This whole situation led me to believe that all Christians were crazy and somewhat delusional because I thought that there was no way that God speaks to people audibly. Nevertheless, I owe many thanks to this man, and the Voice that he heard, for my very existence.

Seeing the Light

Following the death of this minister, a brilliant light visited my dad at church during a Sunday morning church service. A face protruded from inside of the light and thoroughly examined my dad. While growing up, I made fun of him for this story and said that he must've had good flashbacks from the LSD he had taken when he was younger. I didn't believe God existed, nor visit people in the form of light. This experience made my dad feel like he wasn't supposed to leave the congregation, but my mom still had her doubts.

A Family Divided

Nineteen months after my birth, my younger sister was born, and my parents' problems in their marriage escalated, due to my dad's refusal to leave this cultish church. Two years after the minister had died, many people in the church still believed that he was eventually going to come back from the dead. My dad believed that lie, but my mother did not. My mom's final straw in their marriage happened one day when she came home from running errands, and my dad had my siblings and I up against the wall preaching and screaming at us while foaming at the mouth. When he turned around to look at my mom, she

7

saw only one side of his face, which was painted white, and he said, "This side of me wants to do what God wants." Then he turned his head to reveal the other side of his face, which was painted black, and said, "And this side doesn't!" My dad picked up a kitchen knife, looked deep into my mom's eyes and said, "I wonder what it would feel like to put this knife into human flesh." My mom freaked out and immediately filed for divorce.

Shortly after this, my dad was praying on his knees, and my mom came into the room to talk to him, but my dad refused to respond to her. He continued to pray and wouldn't acknowledge my mom whatsoever. Angered by this, she dragged him out of the house, told him it was over, and packed all his belongings into moving boxes. I wanted to move with my dad, so I tried to hide in one of the boxes, but I was immediately found and pulled from the box. I began weeping uncontrollably, because my dad was everything to me when I was a toddler, and it was hard for me to comprehend why he had to leave. This is one of my first and most vivid memories as a child.

Angelic Visitation

After my dad had moved out, my older brother looked out the window, sometime after dusk, and saw three angels standing in our driveway talking to each other. He said that they were lit up like the ghosts of Yoda and Obi-wan Kenobi in the movie series *Star Wars*. This event marked the beginning of many spiritual phenomena that took place in our family that would continue for decades to come.

Childhood Warning

When I was five years old visiting my dad, I remember standing

8

between two paper-white birch trees, and the female "prophet" stooped down, looked me deep in the eyes and said, "Amos, when you're older, they're going to try to mark you with the number 666. Whatever you do, do not accept it!" This memory of her warning meant nothing to me at the time, nor did I remember it until almost 20 years later.

The Big Move

Shortly after my parents' divorce, my mom joined the United States Air Force and was stationed on a military base in central Illinois, six hours away from Michigan. My siblings and I were quite the rowdy bunch and caused my mom a lot of unwanted grief and embarrassment at her new job. We misbehaved a lot around this time, most likely because of our parents' divorce and/or moving so far away from the rest of our family.

A Second Dad

One night while visiting with family in Michigan, my mom was at a bar with her sisters, and a good-looking guy asked her oldest sister to dance. She laughed and told him that she wasn't interested, but that my mom was a good dancer and would likely take him up on his offer. This evening would mark the start of a new romance between him and my mom, to the point that they got married a couple of years later in Illinois. Our stepdad became the dad that we had always wanted because our real dad had stopped coming around and put no effort into seeing us. After my mom had remarried, we saw the genuine love our stepdad had for us, and we eventually called him Dad, gave hugs, and began saying "I love you" to him on a regular basis.

Planting Roots

When I was in the fourth grade, we settled down in the small town of Fisher, which was just 10 miles away from the Air Force base. All of my siblings and I used our stepdad's last name at our new school because we all wanted to associate ourselves with our new dad and disassociate ourselves from the pain of feeling abandoned by our dad. Life was somewhat normal and uneventful until I was in the eighth grade and our family was changed forever. My mom had conceived her fifth child, which was my stepdad's first biological child.

Complications at Birth

The day that my mom went to the hospital to give birth to our little brother, my siblings and I waited with eager anticipation to hear the good news. My oldest sister answered the ringing telephone, and we expected to see joy and excitement on her face, but we saw the opposite instead. With a panicked look and tears rolling down her face, she hung up the phone. We asked her what was going on, and she was too upset to respond. When she gathered the strength, she told us that our new dad had told her that our brother was born completely healthy, but that Mom had died while giving birth. We were all weeping together, wondering what we would do without our mom; she was the glue that held our family together, and we couldn't imagine our lives without her. We all joined hands, in a circle, and began begging God for a miracle. After what seemed like an eternity had passed, but really only minutes, we received another phone call from our dad. He told us that Mom had come back to life, but that she had suffered serious trauma and was unconscious. The joy and pain we went through that day are indescribable, and I could never thank God enough for letting Mom live.

While giving birth to our little brother, my mom's placenta had torn. In a drunken stupor, after coming back from the country club, the doctor performed an emergency hysterectomy on my mom and unknowingly cut the main artery in her leg, then sewed her back up without fixing the mistake. Because of his careless mistake, my mom laid in a pool of her own blood and was given 28 pints of blood, which is nearly three times the amount that the human body holds, to replace all the blood that had leaked from her body. She very clearly recalls what had happened to her before and after she died.

A Glimpse from Beyond

She remembers coming out of her body, with no pain, as she was lying on the operating table, watching the doctors perform surgery on her. She started to ascend out of the operating room, looked down at herself, and asked, "What's happening? Why do I see myself? Why am I here—am I dead?" Then she shot out of the room and was teleported, in what felt like a vacuum, to a long corridor that looked similar to the inside of a horse stable. There were doors on each side of the corridor, as far as her eyes could see. She looked to her side and saw a man standing next to her who stood about seven feet tall, dressed in a garb that closely resembled what a Catholic priest wears. She immediately asked if he was Jesus, and he said, "No." So, she asked if he was God. He replied, "No," began to chuckle, and told her that he was a representative who was there to help her. As they continued talking, she realized that they weren't talking with their mouths but were using telepathy. He explained that nothing was hidden where they were and that everyone there understood each other's thoughts.

Two nine feet tall, illuminated man-like beings came by their side and joined them. Their waist level was at my mom's head, and she was

11

unable to look any higher than that because it felt like a force had held her head down. They shared with my mom some of the mysteries of where they were, as they all moved down the corridor together while levitating a few inches off the ground. She had noticed that behind each door were people wearing different religious apparel that's found throughout the world. Out of curiosity, she asked the man which religion was right. He looked at her and replied, "Every one of these religions holds a portion of the Truth."

The Incredible Alternative

Suddenly, she was in darkness and saw scenes playing on something that was similar to a movie screen, but not the same shape. She literally went into the scenes with the tall man and the two tall beings. Once inside of the first scene, she observed people playing all types of instruments and was mesmerized by the music because it was more beautiful than anything she's ever heard on Earth. She asked the man what it meant, and he replied, "Here, you can play any instrument you'd like. All you have to do is pick it up and play it. You can do anything you'd like here." She went into another scene and found herself standing outside the white picket fence of her dream house. Inside of the house, she saw my new dad holding their newborn son. He looked very peaceful and had a smile on his face. The man looked at her and said, "If this is what you want, you can stay here forever."

Making the Choice

Then he took her into a room that felt like a library, but it had no books. It was a room that was meant for teaching and strategizing on an eternal scale. The tall man in the Catholic garments disappeared, then my mom was encircled by 30 to 40 of the gigantic illuminated beings, and was unable to look at their upper bodies or faces. In the middle of the circle of "beings," just in front of her, was a "super high-tech, rectangular map of the Universe" suspended in the air about five feet above the ground. As they looked into it, movie-type memories and thoughts played in her mind. It felt like they were downloading the information into her brain. Her mouth dropped in amazement when she saw everything they saw, everything they knew, what their plan was, and how it's being played out on Earth. They simultaneously showed her what would happen on Earth if she stayed there, and what would happen if she returned.

After they "downloaded" all the scenes into her mind, everything regarding Earth became a small puzzle piece and slowly slipped back into the map of the Universe; compared to its size, the puzzle piece of this world was nothing more than a dot. After seeing this, without hesitation, she said, "I want to go back!" They told her that if she went back to Earth, she could permanently lose the salvation she had for her sins and that she may never be allowed to come back to that place again. With tears in her eyes, she replied, "I know Jesus will find me again." They informed her that they would block her memory when she came back to Earth and that she would only remember what they thought was important when they deemed it necessary. Again, they warned her that she might not be allowed to come back to that place for making the decision to leave. Nevertheless, She didn't change her mind and was immediately teleported back into her body.

Waking to a New Reality

Suddenly, she woke up in the hospital and noticed a heart monitor beeping, tubes coming out of her mouth, and a nurse standing in the corner of the room. My mom asked, "What happened? Did I get in an accident?" The nurse replied, "No, honey, you had a baby." After regaining her consciousness, we visited my mom in the hospital, and she didn't even recognize who we were. Regardless, we were thrilled to have her back and very thankful that she came back to life. When she finally got out of the hospital, she wasn't the same energetic person that we knew before. She had become very depressed, and for the next seven years, she mostly slept, as she longed to go back to the paradise that she saw when she had died. She felt trapped somewhere between Heaven and Hell and struggled with wanting to commit suicide. One day when I came home from school, my dad was outside their bedroom door yelling, "Don't do it! Don't do it!" I asked him what was going on, and he told me that my mom locked herself in the room and had a gun held to her head. I gave him an odd look, kicked the door open, tackled my mom, and took the gun out of her hand. Another day after school, she sent me to the store to get her medication. When I got back home, she was convulsing on the floor. It was then when we learned that she had developed a seizure condition, in addition to everything else that happened as a result of her losing so much blood after the botched hysterectomy.

CHAPTER 2:
REBEL WITHOUT A CLUE

Young and Dumb

As a teenager, my personality dramatically changed for the worse. I became very foolish, rebellious, and disinterested in school, to the point that I failed almost all of my classes freshman year and got suspended six times. Smoking weed and drinking had become my highest priorities. School became a social outlet, and instead of paying attention in class, I spent my time drawing, flirting with girls, and being the class clown. I had a bad attitude and showed a complete lack of judgment because I never considered the consequences of my actions.

I spent my summer vacations working on farms and saved all the money I'd made. When I got my driver's license, my parents matched what I'd saved and helped me buy my first car. It was much too fast of a vehicle for me because I was a very aggressive driver and had no fear of dying or getting hurt. Very often, I drove around at 120 mph, sometimes with my headlights turned off at night. It was in this car that I'd experience the first of a lifelong series of near-death experiences.

One day, my best friend and I were at the carwash, and I had the hood of my car opened, to polish all of the chrome on the engine. When we got ready to leave, I couldn't find my keys and thought I locked them in the trunk. So I took out my back seat, crawled halfway into the pitch-dark trunk, and flicked a lighter to search for my keys. I saw a trickle of a flame go upwards in the trunk, but I'd neglected to see this as a warning sign and flicked the lighter once again. Suddenly, there was a huge explosion in my face, caused from a spilled gasoline can in my trunk. In a *Matrix*-like fashion, time slowed down as the fire surrounded my face, and somehow I escaped the burning vehicle without any burns or injuries whatsoever. My car, on the other hand, was ruined by the fire. After the firefighters had left the scene, as I dug through the charred belongings in my trunk, I heard a kid say, "Hey, are these your keys?" He'd found them in the engine compartment lying next to the battery. I felt like a complete idiot because I'd misplaced my keys, but more so by my inability to recognize danger when it was literally right in front of my face.

Switching Things Up

My rebellious, party persona continued throughout most of high school, until the summer between my junior and senior year. I clearly remember the night I decided to change: I was at a party passed out drunk on the floor, but I was completely aware of everything that was going on around me. I heard my friends laughing and making fun of me, and felt them walk on my back. I laid there and thought to myself, "These people don't care about me, and the only reason they hang out with me is because I do what they do. Starting tomorrow, I'm changing my friends and my life!" The next day, I stopped smoking weed and completely ignored all of my friends.

I started taking better care of my appearance and reinvented myself before senior year. I cut off my hair, changed my style, had a new group of friends, got straight A's, made the honor roll, joined the football team, and had my first serious girlfriend. Although I'd made many positive changes, dating brought out a side of me that I never knew I had; I'd become extremely jealous and insecure. When my relationship ended, my heart was broken, which took a long time for me to get over it. For the first time in my life, I considered suicide, because I felt like I'd needed another person to make me happy.

A Rude Awakening

My desire to live was restored at the end of my senior year when my friend bought a new car and took me for a drive going 70 mph down an old country road. The car spun out of control, hit a tree stump on the side of the road, flipped three times, and then I blacked out. When I woke up, I was lying on the ground 50 feet from the car, because I didn't wear my seatbelt. I stood up, and it felt like I had a knife stuck in my back. With all my strength, I made myself walk to the road. I was covered with the blood that came from the cuts on my face and back. When I finally made it to the road, I collapsed. I only remember the police arriving and how they covered me with a thermal blanket. When I woke up, I was in a hospital bed and unable to move. I was extremely thankful to God because I didn't die and for regaining my mobility after a couple days of being in the hospital.

After high school, I was very depressed, because I was single and didn't really have a plan for my life. For the lack of a better choice, I tried to join the United States Army. I was still 17 and needed my mom's approval signature on the recruitment papers, but she refused to sign. So, I went with the next best choice and had enrolled at Parkland College. I'd assumed my parents were going to help me pay for tuition, but I was wrong. After I enrolled, my mom said, "Okay—it's time for you to go. I'll help you pack your stuff up and help you pay to get into your own apartment." I responded, "What about college? Aren't you guys help me pay for that?" She replied, "Honey, we can't help you pay for college—I'm sorry, this is all we can do to help you right now." Disappointed, I gratefully accepted my parents' offer for help.

I got the apartment, canceled my college classes, and got a minimum wage job at a local hardware store. I barely made enough money to cover my bills, and there were times that I stole groceries to feed myself. My stealing eventually got me into trouble with the law. A friend and I had stolen three packs of instant lottery tickets, and we ended up turning ourselves in. Then, shortly after that, I got into trouble with the law again for stealing a co-worker's wallet and using his credit cards to go on a shopping spree. I didn't do any jail time for these crimes because I didn't have any prior convictions. However, these crimes were only the beginning of my run-ins with the law.

Hood Rich

I had a personal injury settlement of $12,000, to help cover the medical expenses associated with the car accident I was in and thought that I was rich. I bought a nice car and headed to Michigan to hang out with my cousins; I paid for our hotels, food, and party supplies. I spent all of the settlement money within two months and started stealing again to support myself. One day, our friends asked me to drive them to rob a house, but I didn't really want to go; so I asked my new girlfriend if she cared, secretly hoping she would say no or try to stop me, but she had no issue with it. I reluctantly drove them to rob the house and was completely paranoid as I sat in the car waiting for them. When they got back to the car, they'd stolen money and a gun.

The guys wanted to get a bag of weed, so I drove everyone to the corner store and parked my car. As we sat there waiting, I asked my friend in the backseat to give me his gun, because I had a gut feeling that something bad was about to happen. Three teenage boys approached my car, so I rolled down the windows to talk to them. Suddenly, one of the boys jumped through the passenger side window and stole my wallet. I hopped out of the car, pointed the gun at him, and told him to give it back. He said that he didn't do it and didn't know what I was talking about. Before I knew it, one of his friends had jumped on my back and started wrestling with me, trying to get the gun out of my hands. My friend got out of my car to help me, then I handed him the gun, so I wouldn't get shot fighting over control of the pistol. The guy who robbed me ran into the housing project that was behind the corner store. A few seconds later, a truck full of guys pulled into the parking lot and drove straight towards my car, to trap us in. My friend started to panic, then he pointed the gun at all the guys trying to rob us and told me to get in the car. We got into the car and quickly drove off, and almost hit the truck that was trying to trap us in. As we left the parking lot, my gas light started flashing. I didn't know where I was, so I asked the guys if there was a gas station up the road. They both said that there wasn't and told me to turn around and go back the other way...right back past the store where we were just robbed.

As we approached the corner store, my friend in the back passenger seat started fidgeting with the gun and said, "They're going to pay for what they did!" Then he asked me to roll down the passenger-side window. I told him that he was on the wrong side of the car and to give me the gun. I rolled down the driver's side window, held the gun out the window, and fired three shots into the crowd. The girls in our car started screaming and said that they thought I'd hit someone. I told them to shut up, and that I didn't hit anyone. Then, I turned up Snoop Dogg's song on the radio, "Murder Was the Case."

Unfortunately, the girls were right; I did hit someone when I shot the gun. The bullet had punctured his chest, grazed his heart, and gotten stuck in his back. For the first week after hearing the news, I thought he may have died, and I feared to have to spend the rest of my life in prison. I seriously considered going on the run in Mexico, but thankfully, he lived through the injury. So I turned myself in and was released on bond for a few months in the summer of 1994, as I awaited my trial. Nine days after my twentieth birthday, I took a plea bargain and received a sentence of 4 to 15 years in a state penitentiary for Assault with Intent to Commit Murder.

✿
CHAPTER 3:
IMPRISONMENT TO ENLIGHTENMENT

Failure to Escape

When I first got to prison, I was terrified, because I didn't know what to expect. Surprisingly, it wasn't as bad as I'd imagined. One of the first nights there, my cellmate scored some tobacco, and the only thing we had to smoke it out of was a page from a small Gideon Bible. I didn't feel right about it but justified smoking because the page was blank and didn't have God's Word on it. That night, my cellmate told me that William Shakespeare translated the King James Version of the Bible and then showed me something rather intriguing. He counted so many words in one direction, starting at the beginning of a chapter in Psalms, and pointed at the word "shake." Then, he counted the same number of words in the opposite direction, starting from the back of the chapter, and sure enough, there was the word "sphere." He said that this was proof that this wasn't God's Word but man's, and that William Shakespeare purposely put this in the Bible as his hidden personal signature. This was the first legitimate argument ever presented to me to doubt the words of the Bible, but the attempt was unsuccessful and backfired. As compelling as it was, that night I realized that deep in the heart of me, I was a firm believer in Word of God.

A couple of days later, on the way to my kitchen job, a level 5 inmate tried to intimidate me by talking crap, so I talked smack back and stood up for myself. After my shift was over, while walking back to my cell, he jumped from behind a doorway and knocked me out. After the incident, I had to make a report because I was so bloody from getting hit. I was always looked for loopholes to get out of prison and saw a potential legal issue in this attack. Our level numbers represented our threat levels; the higher the number, the more threatening inmate are deemed. Prisoners were to be segregated by their threat levels. I was a level 1, and the guy who knocked me out was a level 5; legally, I had a case, because we weren't even supposed to be able to cross paths.

One month into my sentence, my girlfriend told me that she was pregnant, so I asked her to marry me. Then I told her I'd find a way to get out to be there when our baby was born. I headed to the law library and started searching for anything to substantiate my case. I soon discovered a case that I could use as the basis for my lawsuit; a case where a low-level inmate was released from prison because he was sexually assaulted by a higher-level inmate. Although this attack was different than mine, the lightbulb went off in my head, and I thought I'd found my ticket to freedom. In my mind, all I had to do was change my story to match the case I'd found and get my family to believe it, so they'd hire me an attorney...and I'd be free.

In the new rendition of my story, I'd claimed that when I knocked out, I was sexually assaulted. I felt horrible for lying to my family but was desperate to be there for the birth of my first child. I told the counselor on my cellblock the new version of what happened. Unexpectedly, they gave me a medical examination and said it didn't look like anything had happened. They asked me to take a lie detector test, and I started to panic because I knew there was no way that I could pass it. When they summoned me for questioning, I told them I'd became a Christian, forgave the guy, dropped the charges against him, and decided to leave it in God's hands. My ticket to freedom was gone, and I was utterly humiliated. I had to come to terms with the fact that prison was where I'd spend the next few years.

My girlfriend came to visit me, and we talked about setting up arrangements to get married at the prison. Once she left, I never heard from her again, presumably because of the lie I told. From that point forward, every phone call I made was denied and every letter got mailed back to me with a "Return to Sender" stamp on it. After nine months of being in prison, I heard that she gave birth to our daughter. Shortly afterward, I started a court case to have the state administer a DNA test to see if our new baby was truly mine. The test came back positive—I was the father of our newborn daughter.

While in prison, I lived a double life. I'd go to church but sold drugs to support my weed habit. I had one of the highest paying jobs as a sign painter and math tutor, making $75 a month. Because time went by so incredibly slow, I worked out and studied Algebra, Geometry, Trigonometry, Calculus, Latin, and Physics, to prepare myself for college when I got out. I read the Bible three times, even though it made no sense to me.

A Taste of Freedom

After three years in prison, I went to a corrections center in a suburb of Detroit. I was still a prisoner but was allowed to get a real job in the community. I worked as a server at a Mexican restaurant and started sending money to my daughter's mother to help out. Because of this, she allowed me to finally meet my daughter for the first time. I left the corrections center on a two-hour pass to shop at K-mart and visit with my daughter. The center had a zero-tolerance policy which required me to have a receipt from the store within fifteen minutes of returning to my cell. I lost track of time because I was enjoying the time I got to spend with my daughter. I rushed to the cash register and asked everyone in line if I could please go ahead of them, but no one would let me, which made me eight minutes late when I returned to the center. Because of the policy, I was sent back to prison for eight months; one month per minute that I was late. At the time, this day turned out to be the best day of my life because I got to see my daughter for the first time...yet it was the worst day of my life because I got sent back to prison for eight more months.

Free at Last

After eight extremely long months, I was released from prison and landed a job at a restaurant in Flint, Michigan. I met a girl who worked there with me, and we started dating shortly after. Eventually, we decided to enroll in college together and rented a house together that was close to campus. Once school started, I began to desire to be with other women, which led me to cheat on my girlfriend much too often. Things got complicated once I found out she was pregnant. I was dumbfounded by it because she was on the pill. Despite my doubts, I asked her to marry me. Her parents weren't happy about it and wanted her to have an abortion. She claimed that she called the clinic and they told her that she only had 12 weeks so that it was now too late to make the decision. Having my doubts, I called the clinic to verify, but I found out we really had 25 weeks to make the decision. I hung up the phone and was enraged because I felt like she lied to me and was trying to trap me into the relationship. A few days later, I paid for her to have an abortion and ended our engagement.

While all this was happening, I was still on parole. My parole was supposed to last for two years, but my parole officer told me that he was letting me off a year early because I was a model parolee. With this good news, I decided to go back to Illinois to attend college and reunite with my family. Although our engagement had ended, we were still dating. I told my girlfriend that I wasn't taking her with me and that I'd cheated on her. I'd assumed that my honesty would've made her agree that a breakup was needed. However, she responded with something I didn't expect at all; instead of wanting to leave me, she said that she forgave me and wanted to work things out and have a fresh start together in Illinois. Convinced by her love for me, I had a change of heart, and we made the move together. Had I not been let off parole early, nothing you're reading from this point forward would have happened, which is a crucial point to remember.

Darkness in Illinois

Before we'd arrived in Illinois, my brother started reading the Bible and had a frightening experience in our soon-to-be apartment. One night, he suddenly awoke to an overwhelmingly heavy, dark entity on his back. Paralyzed, unable to breathe, and in a desperate panic, he yelled, "Get off me, motherfu#%er!" but nothing happened. Not knowing what else to do, he shouted, "Jesus!" Immediately, the entity lifted off him, and he could move and breathe freely again. At the same moment, he heard a loud bang in the dining room. When he got up to see what made the noise, he found that his Bible had been thrown off the shelf and onto the floor. At the time, I didn't think much of the story and was completely unaware that in the months and years to come, the same dark presence that attacked my brother would come taunt me, too.

My brother moved out of the apartment where this strange phenomenon happened, and we took it over. The newfound freedom of being off parole, able to do whatever I wanted, led to me partying with my college friends, cheating often and ultimately becoming the worst version of myself; I was excessively promiscuous, self-absorbed, vain, selfish, cruel, evil, and beyond heartless towards my girlfriend. I broke up with her during a horrible fight that ended in her saying, "I can't take this anymore! I'm leaving you in God's hands!" At the time, I was clueless about how profound and prophetic her statement was. Yet, in retrospect, I see it clear as day. Right after our fight, my cousin from Michigan called me and said, "Amos, you need to come to Detroit; this is going to change your life!" He didn't give me the details of what he meant, but it was enough to spark his my curiosity, so I headed there right away.

The New Millennium

It was the Millennial New Year's Eve, everyone was partying like it was 1999, and there wasn't a global computer crash, but something started happening that led to my life and person being transformed forever. I quickly learned what my cousin was talking about—the rave scene: huge techno parties that took place in the abandoned warehouses in downtown Detroit with a few thousand teens and twenty-somethings all doped up on LSD, Ecstasy, and nitrous oxide. I began witnessing things that I'd never seen before—things that made me question everything I'd previously known about life. I remember taking a hit of nitrous, and everyone at the party, almost three thousand people, turned their heads in unison and looked me directly in the eye. It appeared as if "something" was pulling the strings of everyone in the building, causing them to look at me at the exact same time, almost like they were puppets. I've tried to explain this

26

experience, but it's been difficult for me to find the words. When I watched the movie *Inception*, my jaw dropped when I saw a scene portrayed in this film when everyone stopped and looked the main character in the eyes at the same time; it was nearly identical to what I didn't know what kept happening to me. I was very intrigued each time it happened, as I contemplated its meaning. However, started making me question my understanding of reality altogether.

I couldn't go back to school in Illinois and pretend I didn't see what I saw in Detroit. I felt like I had to keep pressing in and figure out what was happening. Living the rave lifestyle was expensive; instead of being one of the crowd, going broke by partying too much, I joined my cousin and became a drug dealer at the raves. I took every dollar I had and bought three vials of the best liquid LSD I'd ever taken. I used my first profits to move my daughter and her mom out of her ex-boyfriend's house and into a townhouse. He and I bumped heads because we both wanted to date my daughter's mother; the situation escalated to a point where one of us was likely to kill the other because we were both very violent people.

I Saw the Light

A week into the new millennium, I went to my dad's house and decided to dose myself. As I looked around his living room, I said, "Man, this is gonna be boring, there's nothing to get good visuals from," because he didn't have any oil paintings or textured ceilings, which would have appeared to come alive and swirl around when I took LSD. I looked over to a spot on the floor and realized that it was where my daughter was conceived on the day I went to prison. The very second this dawned on me, a bright, brilliant, colorful light, unlike anything I've ever seen before, illuminated a picture on the wall and animated it in colors that resembled a mixture of a computer screen and sunlight, but much more vibrant. [There's a copy of the picture located at the end of this chapter.] I saw a lamb running for its life on the side of a cliff; as the dirt fell from beneath its feet, I lost my breath, because I thought it was going to fall to its death. Right then, the image of Jesus in the picture bent over, picked up the lamb, set it safely on solid ground, and fell off the cliff after He saved its life. I knew that the light's appearance was more than drugs because there aren't words nearly powerful enough to even describe what I saw. I stood up to my feet, and as the brilliant light still shined, it was crystal clear to me that I was in the presence of God. I looked around the room, and said, "God, what are you trying to say, that Jesus died for us or what?" but I heard no reply. Puzzled, I said aloud, "God, what are you trying to say? Are we all going to Heaven or what?" After these words had left my mouth, the light retracted back into the picture to the size of a small pinhole, stayed that way for about three seconds, and then disappeared. Tears ran down my face, and I was instantly sober. With a huge smile on my face, I said aloud, "OH MY GOD! IT'S TRUE! The whole Bible is True! Jesus really died on the cross and came back from the dead, and I was just visited by Him!" All my life, I'd thought Christians were crazy and foolish for believing such fairytale nonsense. I'd made fun of my dad for His claim that he was visited by a light at church when he was 25, but there I was at the same age and was just visited by the same light in his living room!

Standing in amazement, I wiped the tears from my eyes and said aloud, "God, now that I know You're real, I'll do whatever You want me to do." Being the young and naïve believer that I was, I had the bright idea to take the drugs and picture to raves, dose people for free, and let them see the light I saw. However, right then, my conscience let me know that this wasn't what God wanted me to do. So, I said aloud, "What do You expect me to do then?" After saying this, I heard my conscience say, "I want you to take all the drugs and flush them down the toilet." I chuckled and said, "God, this is everything I have. If I flush this down the toilet, I won't have any money for gas, food, child support, or bills. So, if I do this, You're going to have to take care of me, because I'll have nothing and have no plan besides this." With hesitation and fear of having nothing to my name, I squeezed the vials one by one into the toilet and flushed it all down the drain. Then I said, "Ok. There You go. Please help me because now I have nothing."

Overcoming Evil

Shortly after I flushed my stash down the toilet, I noticed something very strange that I'd never seen before: my driver's license number contained six 6's in a row. After seeing this, I remembered the warning given to me as a child, "When you get older, they're going to try to mark you with the number 666. Whatever you do, do not accept it." Provoked by this memory, I visited the DMV a few months later to get a new license number and discovered the only way to do this was to change my name. I attempted to rename myself in court, but the judge denied the request because of my criminal history and told me to come back in five years. To my surprise, the State of Michigan passed legislation that made all driver's license numbers permanent and unchangeable. I knew the numbers on my license weren't the mark of the beast, but I refused to identify myself with them. At the time, I had no idea that this would soon become one of the biggest battles of my entire life.

That night, I read the Bible, and for the first time in my life, every word I read made sense. The first lesson I learned was how I could overcome evil by doing good. God made it clear that He wanted me to make things right with my daughter's stepdad. I don't know how, but that night the violent man that I once was disappeared. God gave me an assignment, and I instinctively knew exactly what to do. I had three concert tickets to a Britney Spears concert to take my daughter, her mother, and I the day immediately following my encounter with God lighting up the picture on the wall. However, my conscience told me to give the tickets to my daughter's stepdad, with the keys to my dad's new car, and some cash to spend at the concert, and let him take my place.

The day of the concert, as I walked into my daughter's house, her stepdad led me into a bedroom, grabbed me by the throat, and lifted me into the air. Unable to breathe, I reached into my pocket, grabbed the tickets, handed them to him, and struggled to say the words, "Here are the tickets to the concert. I want you to take my daughter and her mom." He let me down, let go of my throat, took the tickets from my hand, and gave me the strangest look I've ever seen anyone give me. I took the car keys and cash out of my pocket and handed them to him. He stood there, confused because he knew that I would've usually never let anyone manhandle me like that without a fight, and my response took him completely by surprise.

What the Hell?

Although I was no longer a violent man or drug dealer, I was still intrigued by the spiritual encounters that I had with drugs. I went to my cousin's house a couple of days later and took another hit of LSD. Shortly afterward, I looked around the room and realized that I'd wronged everyone in the room, at some point in the recent past. I felt very guilty inside, and it seemed like I was being judged. Suddenly, two big, evil looking hands about three feet tall, attached to old, rusty chains came out of nowhere and started dragging me into Hell. As they were pulling me in, I started screaming, "Jesus, Jesus!!!" and immediately, the hands let me go and retreated to Hell. It took a long time for me to recover from this experience, as Hell became very real to me that night.

Strangely enough, my aunt had a parallel experience in the same house a few days after mine, minus the drugs. She had a vision where her house had transformed into a dimly lit cave, and a big rock took the place of where her kitchen should've been. On top of the rock sat Jesus. My aunt asked him, "What's going on? Where am I, and why does it smell like sulfur?" Jesus told her that they were sitting at the gates of Hell...in the very place where I was pulled in by the monstrous hands attached to chains. In a panic, she said, "Please don't make me go to Hell!" He replied, "Wherever you go, I will be with you. You won't go through anything you can't handle." Suddenly, the cave disappeared, and she was standing alone in her house, completely unsure of what had just happened. Her house became a very symbolic place for us both, as we had parallel experiences in the same place that seemed to validate each other and appeared to be much more than a coincidence.

After seeing the horrifying things I've seen, most people would've permanently dropped the drug, but I, on the other hand, did not. In my mind, enduring these spiritual attacks felt like I was a modern-day David fighting Goliath. The chances of me going to Hell seemed worth the risk. Looking back, I can see that surviving these attacks was part of my purpose and mission in life, but I don't suggest, nor do I any longer practice, doing drugs to find God or have spiritual encounters.

Had it not been for the Holy Spirit comforting me inside of my heart, reassuring me that I was His, I probably would've ended up in a psychiatric ward.

Saved from Life in Prison

Around the same time, I went to my cousin's house and thought he was having a party because there were fifteen to twenty cars in the driveway, but I was wrong; the cars were all belonged to DEA agents and local undercover officers. When I got out of my car, they searched me and went through my vehicle. They'd been following us because they knew that we'd sold drugs at raves. As they tore my car apart, they took out my satchel, and found only a Bible sitting in the place where my drugs used to be. Had it been a week earlier, there would've been enough drugs in my satchel to put me in prison for the rest of my life. At that moment, I understood that every day from that point forward was an undeserved gift from God. As a result of Him visiting me as light at my dad's house, prompting me to flush my stash down the toilet, I experienced first-hand what it meant to literally be "saved" from myself. Unfortunately for my cousin, he was caught with his drugs and did four years in a federal prison.

This is the picture that God lit up on the wall and animated to help save me from going back to prison for the rest of my life

CHAPTER 4:
THE INESCAPABLE MISTAKE

The Circle of Life

To flee the spiritual attacks in Michigan and regain my sense of reality, I moved back to Illinois and spent a lot of time with my family. I lived with my best friend at the time, who was in his late 30's and the father of a beautiful daughter. She and I were very flirty with each other, which made me feel conflicted within myself—my desire for his daughter and the life God wanted for me were complete opposites. One night while everyone was sleeping, we took things to a level we shouldn't have. I was inwardly crushed by the feelings of guilt and betrayal towards my best friend. The next night as I drove home from work, I turned the radio to a classical music station and noticed that the horns and trumpets seemed like they were coming from inside my chest. It felt like my heart was beating along to the music. Overwhelmed by this experience, tears rolled down my face, and a bright shooting star flashed across the sky. Years later, after I realized that this was the first night I felt the Holy Spirit in my heart, and this phenomenal encounter showed me that God forgave one of the worst mistakes of my life.

A few nights later at a karaoke bar, I heard someone sing an eerie rendition of the song "The Cat's in the Cradle." When I looked at the guy singing, I realized that years earlier my best friend, brother, and I had severely beat him up, to the point that he was hospitalized for a broken nose and ribs; for messing around with my sister, who was several years younger than him. I was deeply convicted by the strange coincidence of what had happened with my best friend's daughter. I began to feel very remorse for what we did to him, so when he got off the stage, I apologized and asked for his forgiveness. He let me know that he had forgiven us long ago. I told him about all the spiritual attacks I'd been through. He responded by telling me that he'd been trying to break two brothers away from worshipping the devil, whose grandfather allegedly wrote the Satanic Bible. Then he said, "Amos, I think God wants you to come with me and tell these guys everything that happened to you." Without delay, we headed straight to the boys' apartment. When we walked through the door, I was dumbfounded because I recognized the oldest brother: he was the boyfriend of my best friend's daughter. All things considered, I felt like a complete hypocrite because I knew what nobody else did in the room.

Gone in an Instant

I should've taken that night as a warning to stop messing around with her. However, within a few days, we continued to dabble in our secret relationship. We were careless, and her stepmom started catching on that something was happening between us. As I headed upstairs on my way to bed, both she and her stepmom saw what they described as a "black smoke or shadow" follow me up the stairs. It was similar to what my brother described that attacked him in his apartment. The next morning, I got a phone call from her stepmom; she told me that when she asked her stepdaughter if anything had happened between us, she said that I sexually assaulted her. Then, her stepmom told me that the police were on their way. I packed up my belongings and headed to another friend's house. Within minutes, my mom had arrived and was crying uncontrollably, infuriated because she believed that the allegations against me were true. I told her my version of the story and concluded that the accusations likely happened because her stepmom was suspicious and she didn't want to look bad to her family. I pleaded with my mom to believe me because I was innocent and refused to go to jail for something that I did not do. Sobbing uncontrollably, I was crushed by this situation, because my world crumbled right before my eyes. I told my mom goodbye and drove away toward Texas to escape the law; my world and reputation were crushed. I wept for hours because it felt like I just died and was never going to see my family again. The allegations flew through my family like wildfire—nearly 300 people believed that I did it. News traveled to my daughter's mother, as well, and she said I wouldn't be allowed to see my daughter ever again. I couldn't help but feel that I was finally reaping what I'd sown years earlier for accusing someone of sexually assaulting me, in a desperate attempt to get out of prison.

I never made it to Texas but ended up in Missouri at the house of my childhood bestfriend. After a week of being there, I received a phone call from my mom, and she told me that everyone back in Illinois was starting to believe my version of the story because the girl's story kept changing. Hope was birthed inside of me that this would all be behind me one day, so instead of going to Texas I headed back to Michigan. Even though I had hope, I'd successfully destroyed my life by not listening to my gut instinct. The only option I saw to restore my life was by fasting and seeking God's help and direction. I fasted for two weeks at my aunt's house by not eating any food for two weeks and journaled the whole experience.

Seeking Direction

During the fast, My aunt and I were talking on the porch one night when suddenly two lights, the same brightness, and size of stars, whizzed through the trees and stopped directly in front of us about one hundred yards away. In amazement, I looked over to my aunt and asked if she was seeing what I was seeing and she did. I'm not sure why, but I began to speak to them in my head and asked, "Do you hear me?" They began moving up and down, presumably indicating that they could hear my thoughts. I asked more questions, and they continued to move up and down to answer yes and side to side for no. My aunt and I weren't the only ones having experiences with these balls of light. One the size of a golf ball flew into my cousin's room, around the same time. It hovered two feet in front of my cousin's boyfriend's face and examined him. It moved to the other side of the bed in front of my cousin's face, stayed there for a few seconds, and then disappeared into her mouth. And no, we weren't on drugs.

I've often wondered why we had these experiences and tried to discern their meaning. The best interpretation that I have for these encounters is that they're visual representations of what the Holy Spirit does. Just as the light disappeared into my cousin's mouth, the Holy Spirit comes to live inside of your heart and communicates with you there. Just as the lights were reading my thoughts and moved along with them, the Holy Spirit will come to live in your heart, read your mind, and "beat" what you pay attention to in your heart. Not to say that the Holy Spirit is a genie and will give you all the answers you need, but He will help you through the tough times and comfort you from within.

The Indwelling

The night after the experience, something phenomenal happened to me that paralleled these visual manifestations. I went outside and began praying on my knees. I felt a massive force of energy inside my body, pulsing and gyrating in my heart area, not in a mystical sense, but inside of my actual heart. I prayed internally, "Jesus, is that you?" The "force" inside my body started moving up and down to answer "Yes." Then I asked if I needed to stay in the kneeling position, and the "energy" inside me began moving side to side, indicating an answer of "No." I asked many questions and wrote them all down in my journal, as crazy as it sounds. However, this phenomenon of feeling Him answer questions inside of my heart only happened on this one occasion. As I've said, the Holy Spirit isn't a genie or a magic eight ball. Ever since then, I've only felt God's Spirit make His presence known inwardly and not actually give yes or no answers as He did that night.

In response to God revealing Christ living inside of my heart, the devil intensified his level of attacks on my mind and identity. While journaling everything that happened, my aunt took a photograph of me with a disposable camera. When the film was developed, she told me that one photo showed several demons with evil grins on their faces surrounding me. This is significant because of what I was writing in my journal at the time she took the photograph. I was naively trying to discern my eternal destiny; I wrote, "Am I a child of God or am I going to hell because of the 6's on my driver's license? Is this the reason I've suffered so many spiritual attacks?" To determine the answer to this question, I made the if/then statements, "If I'm a child of God, I will marry the girl that I first dated after prison, because only God could make it happen, and this will be His sign. If this doesn't happen, then the 6's on my license mean that I'm going to Hell." As a lost soul trying to make sense of everything I'd been through, I didn't realize the power of these words until years later because they had literally put me into a mental prison that I couldn't escape. I know this sounds like lunacy and foolishness, but these if/then statements affected all my future decisions and became the biggest battle of my life, as I struggled to find my true identity for years to come.

Towards the end of the fast that I mentioned earlier, the attacks started getting unbearable to the point that it felt like I was beginning to lose my mind. One night, two surprise visitors showed up; my older sister and female cousin from Zion, Illinois. The girls came because they had felt a strong, undeniable urge that God wanted them to drop what they were doing and drive to my aunt's house in Michigan. The mental anguish showed on my face, which made them realize that God had sent them there to help me. My sister told me to pack up my things and come with them to Zion. It seemed like I was being rescued from an inescapable and agonizing situation without even asking for help.

The Voices in Zion

When we arrived in Zion, I met my cousin's boyfriend, who was deeply into studying the Bible. He told me that he'd been praying for the sons and daughters of God that needed help learning about their true identity and purpose to be drawn to him for teaching. That night, he taught me that Christ forgives our sins and that those who believe in Him become the adopted children of God. During our studies, I got distracted, because I continued to gravitate towards the verses about the mark of the beast: 666. Once my cousin's boyfriend had noticed me doing this, he said, "I'm teaching you about Christ and all He did for you, and you keep studying about the mark of the beast!" I replied that the sixes on my license made me question whether God viewed me as His own and that I was trying to figure it out. Then he said, "I'm showing you who you are—you're a child of God! Those numbers mean nothing!" After he'd made that statement, I asked if he agreed that what I felt in my heart was the Holy Spirit or not. He replied, "No, what you feel is not the Holy Spirit, it's a demon—and you're possessed!"

Within minutes of our conversation, he attempted to cast a demon out of me. Afterward, I went outside by myself and began crying out to God, sobbing like a baby, "Please, God, let me be a part of your Kingdom! I don't want to go to Hell, and I want nothing to do with the sixes on my license! I do not accept them! I love You!" I appreciated that my cousin's boyfriend was trying to help me, but I didn't agree with him that the Holy Spirit in me was a demon. I knew there was no way a demon would comfort my heart and give me reassurance that I belonged to God, immediately after the countless spiritual attacks that tried to convince me that I was going to Hell.

A few nights after this happened, I had a dream that Britney Spears kissed me. I pushed her off me and said, "We shouldn't be doing this." She kissed me again, but her tongue went quickly in and out of my mouth, like the tongue of a snake. The dream quickly progressed, and we began doing other things, which instantly woke me up. As I laid there with my eyes wide open, I experienced the same paralysis and inability to breathe that my older brother suffered years earlier in Illinois; it felt like a thousand-pound, dark presence was on my back. Able to see but unable to move, I heard what sounded like fifty voices whispering back and forth very quickly to each other, next to my right ear. As I looked around the room trying to figure out what was going on, I could only understand one thing—one of the voices whispered, "He thinks we sound like him." Right after hearing this, I gathered up enough strength and said, "Jesus!" After His name had left my lips, the dark presence was gone, and I was immediately able to move and breathe again. At that same moment, on the other side of the house my cousin woke up to the sound of many voices screeching and screaming outside her bedroom window. This presence must have been the same dark entity that taunted my brother in our old apartment. This phenomenon was similar to what I've heard described happening during sleep paralysis but was much stronger and darker of a force or being.

The Matrix of Time

I left Zion shortly after this experience and headed back to Michigan. On New Year's Eve of 2001, my cousin invited me to a party, and my dad invited me to attend a church service with him. I, of course, chose the first option. When I arrived at the party, my cousin held out his hands, in one was a blue pill and in the other was a red pill. He then asked me, "Democrat or Republican?" I chose Republican and took the red pill, which made this night feel like the Matrix. As the time approached midnight, fear crept its way into my mind because I felt that I'd made the wrong decision and thought I should've gone to church with my dad instead. I asked my cousin if he could get everyone to move their cars out of the driveway so I could leave. He tried to calm me down, insisting that no one wanted to move their cars. As I walked through the party, bits and pieces from everyone's conversations started blending into one narrative that tried to convince me that I was going to Hell. In a state of panic, I went into the bathroom, put my fingers in my ears, got on my knees, and began quoting Scriptures to myself about salvation that I'd learned in Zion.

Doing this was enough to build up my faith, stop the panic attack, and help me feel like I wasn't losing my mind. At the very moment I'd regained my confidence, someone knocked on the bathroom door, so I stood up and walked back into the party.

Two seconds before midnight, as I stood in a circle with ten of my guy friends, the techno music in the party changed into an eery twinkling sound, and everyone in the room froze in time, stuck in stationary positions, except for me. It seemed as though they were more like soulless puppets than actual people. I noticed that all my friends appeared to be motionless reflections of myself, from different years and phases in my life. As this realization came to my mind, I heard an old school phone ring that sent chills down my spine because there was no phone in the room. It felt like it was time to meet my Maker and face the consequences for all the wrong things I did in my life. It literally felt like any second I was going to be in Hell. Fearing what was going to happen next, I covered my eyes for two to three seconds, and quietly whispered to myself, "Man, Satan is messing with my head." When I took my hands away from my eyes, everyone in the party had disappeared, and I was left standing there completely by myself. I covered my eyes again and said under my breath, "I wish Satan was here right now, I'd put him in his place!" That very second, someone tapped me on the shoulder. I took my hands away from my face, opened my eyes and saw a guy standing next to me; we were the only people in the whole party. He looked me deep in the eyes and said, "What's up man? Let's talk." It honestly felt like I was talking directly to Satan himself. Ironically, when I had the opportunity, rather than being courageous and putting him in his place, I was afraid and didn't say a word. He walked me over to a couch, we sat down, and he did all the talking, but I didn't listen to anything he said. Within a minute, I looked up, and the party was full of people again.

After everyone had reappeared, I stood up and quickly walked into the other room. I sat down on the floor with my head in my hands and tried to figure out what had just happened. A girl I barely knew sat down on the floor next to me, put her hand on my shoulder, and said, "Don't worry Amos, the Holy Spirit is going to get you through this." I looked at her in amazement, because I didn't tell anyone what had just happened, and we'd never talked about God before. I sat in the same spot for the rest of the night, replaying what had happened in my mind over and over, trying to figure out how it was even possible. At the crack of dawn, the sunshine crept through the windows, and everyone was getting ready to go home. Still sitting in the same spot from the night before, I heard the guy who tapped me on the shoulder say in a loud voice in the other room, "Dude, I was Satan at the party last night!" Chills went down my spine, because I didn't tell anybody what I'd seen and what he said seemed to be more than just a crazy coincidence. Immediately after hearing this, I got up and left the party. This frightening experience deeply twisted my sense of reality and made me feel that everyone on Earth wasn't real. I felt like my whole life was not what it appeared, and that everyone was either part of a grand illusion or characters in the Matrix of ultimate reality, designed for the sole purpose of informing me that I'd be spending eternity in Hell.

❀
CHAPTER 5:
RAILROAD TO REDEMPTION

Sorrowful Regret

Soon after my *Matrix* experience, I had a dream that shook me to the core and further convinced me of what I thought God wanted me to do. It began with me flying into a cafeteria, and a man, who sat at the table, told me, "I'm going to show you where you're going, just do me a favor and don't ask me how you got there." Immediately, I flew into a dark portal and continued traveling at a very rapid speed. In horror, I began yelling over and over, "Jesus! Jesus! Jesus!" After exiting the portal, I ended up at my ex-girlfriend's parents' house, standing next to her nephew. With joy, I said, "This must be where Jesus wants me to be!" I noticed my dad's car parked in their driveway with a baby carrier strapped into its back seat. My ex-girlfriend walked up to me, and I gave her a confused look because I didn't know what was going on; then, she giggled and told me that we were together. I pointed to the baby seat in my dad's car, and she said that we had our baby. I dropped to my knees and wept uncontrollably, which woke me up out of my sleep, and I continued to cry for more than two hours because it felt like the baby in the car seat was the child I'd aborted. For the first time since making the decision, I had remorse for killing my own child. Although this dream brought me to this sobering realization, I came out with the notion that God wanted me to be with my ex.

Abortion wasn't the only regret I dealt with at this time in my life. I was also severely depressed because I'd betrayed my best friend. I felt that I'd made the biggest mistake of my life and couldn't escape the repercussions of going against my conscience. Although I knew God had forgiven me, I didn't; feeling so unfaithful made me lose my desire to live. One night after crying myself to sleep over these feelings, I had a profound dream in which my best friend's daughter and I were flying freely outside of a shopping center. I followed her into the mall, as we both flew thru its exterior wall and ended up inside. As we passed thru the wall, I heard what sounded like twenty voices grumbling amongst themselves, arguing that this act wasn't allowed. In return, I said, "If it's God's will, then it's going to happen!" We flew through another wall, and there was a moment of darkness before we came out through the other side. Again, I heard the voices saying that this wasn't allowed. I replied the same thing as before—if it's God's will, then it's going to happen!

The Little Boy

As we flew into the third wall, rather than a flash of black, I found myself in a place of permanent darkness. The voices continued saying that this wasn't allowed. Suddenly, I heard a young boy in the distance cheerfully say, "I'm here to show him that he's faithful!" The other voices angrily protested, still insisting that this wasn't allowed and was somehow breaking the rules. Despite their objections, the boy repeated himself twice more, each time sounding as though He got closer and closer. When he arrived directly in front of me, the other voices stopped altogether and then He said, "I'm here to show you that you're faithful!" I replied with a simple, "Okay." He then said, "I'm here to show you that you're faithful! I'm the eternal part of you, and I live in your heart! Just as you were born from below, I was born from above, and I'm here to show you that you're faithful! I'm going to ask you a question, but you need to understand that how you answer could change everything for you." I again replied, "Okay." Then, He asked, "All I have to ask you is this: are you willing to go the next step that awaits you after you leave this life?" I immediately responded, "Yes!" Inquisitively, He asked, "Are you sure? Because if you make this decision, you may never see your family or daughter again." Without hesitation, I replied, "Yes, I'm ready, let's go."

After answering His question the second time, I thought I'd suddenly find myself at the next step in life, whatever that may be. However, I remained alone in the darkness, and it seemed as though the boy had abandoned me altogether. In an attempt to maintain my peace, I said aloud to myself, "Oh my God, this IS the next step—this must be Hell! I can remember everything bad I've ever done. The eternal part of me must've gone to Heaven, and I'm stuck here by myself, forever. I'm not going to freak out. Everything's going to be okay, and I'm going to be here forever, so I might as well not panic." I began to hear crickets chirping in the darkness, which made me wonder if I was outside. Suddenly, I felt the sensation of being in my body and it appeared as if I was lying down. I opened my eyes and saw the picture on the wall that had lit up, which saved me from going back to prison. I jumped off my dad's couch, and cheerfully proclaimed, "Yes! I'm alive! I'm alive!" That morning, the feelings of depression and unfaithfulness left me for good. From that day forward, when I hear crickets, I hone in on one of them and feel it beat on inside your chest, as I continue to familiarize myself with the eternal part of me living inside of my heart.

Before this dream, my decisions to kill my unborn child and betray my best friend, made me feel at the core of my being that I was an unfaithful and disloyal person who deserved nothing good in life. These feelings overwhelmed me to the point that life became unbearable and I'd lost my desire to live. However, God used this dream to confirm that it was Him that I'd been feeling in my heart and that despite the foolish decisions of my past, that He viewed me as a faithful adopted child of God and was unquestionably His. I woke up, excited to be alive, and the feelings of betrayal and unfaithfulness permanently left me. This dream birthed one of the most liberating moments of my entire life, as I no longer wallowed in the guilt and shame I used to feel on a daily basis.

He was a Carpenter

Around the same time, a friend had offered me a job as a carpenter, building new homes and apartment buildings. Believing that I was above this line of work and viewing "those kinds of people" as uneducated, I quickly turned down the position. Later that evening, I heard my conscience say, "Jesus was a carpenter—what makes you think you're any better than Him?!" In complete agreement with my conscience and a desire to follow the example of Jesus, I took the job and began working the next morning. Being a carpenter was extremely challenging both physically and mentally, mostly because my superiors required me to carry heavy loads of lumber and were verbally abusive. I was called all kinds of vulgar names because I was the low man on the totem pole. They treated me as a slave, showing no respect nor dignity. Daily, I would question why I continued to put up with such a horrible work environment. However, as much as I hated my job, I stuck with it, because I thought that this was what God wanted me to do.

I remember one day at work when my perspective completely

changed, as I came to understand the sufferings of Christ in a whole new light. As I carried a 40-foot floor joist by myself, I had a feeling similar to being stabbed in my knee with a knife which made me scream and fall to the ground. As I was lying there, I saw images in my mind of Jesus carrying His cross. Thinking about His brutal suffering gave me a sense of inner strength and made the pain more bearable; despite my excruciating pain, I stood back up and continued to do my job. Later that day, I was unable to swing my hammer because every time I did, it felt as though I was nailing Jesus to the cross. Right after this happened, I quit my job and decided to leave Michigan, because I thought it was a spiritually dark place for me geographically.

Up the Stairs

I moved to a suburb of Dallas, Texas, began working as a server, and life seemed relatively normal for the first couple of months. By moving to a new state, I thought I'd finally escaped the spiritual attacks and flashbacks that had previously haunted me. That is until it all began again on the night of my 28th birthday when I had two separate "happenings" that both involved staircases. The first experience happened as I was traveling up an escalator of a multi-story mall in downtown Dallas, as a man stood on the step immediately behind me and seemed almost to be on my shoulder. I had no idea why he was standing so close to me because no one else was on the escalator. I looked back at him and realized he was nearly seven feet tall, had white hair and brilliant blue, glowing eyes, unlike any I've seen before. I asked him, "What's your name?" He smiled, looked at me deep in the eye and said, "Michael." I replied, "Oh," and was completely weirded out and felt a little uncomfortable because somehow I knew that he was an angel appearing as a man. We rode the escalator to the very top, and he stood right next to me the entire way up. In any other

49

context, I would find this man's behavior strange, but there was something mysteriously calming about his presence. My suspicion that an angel had followed me up the escalator didn't make sense at the time, but in retrospect what happened to me later that night as I headed down a flight of stairs put it all into perspective.

Down the Stairs

The second experience happened after I met up with some friends at a local club that night to celebrate my birthday. As we pressed our way through the crowd of people dancing to the rhythm of electronic house music, I recalled a perplexing question that my older brother had once asked me, "When you were at the bar, have you ever noticed that it looks like people were dancing on the edge of the pits of hell?" As I pondered his words and watched everyone around me primitively bounce to the sensual beat, I finally understood his question, because I was witnessing it with my eyes. Lost in this thought, I followed my friends up to the rooftop bar on the second level, where the music was more upbeat, and the vibe wasn't as dark. Because of this, we spent the rest of the evening hanging out up there. The entire night the music on both levels was purely instrumental and without lyrics. However, as we headed downstairs to leave, the moment my foot touched the enclosed stairwell, a loud, eerie, peculiarly timed voice came over the beat and said, "You know what time it is!" and slowly started to countdown from 10. As I walked down the stairwell, I noticed flames painted on the walls and a sign that read, "Last chance to turn back!" The countdown continued, "9-8-7," as I turned the next bend and saw another sign that read, "We've been waiting for you!" As I heard, "6-5-4," the music downstairs began to blend with the music upstairs, reminding me of my brother's question about the pits of Hell. When the countdown hit "3-2-1..." time came to a screeching halt, every head in the stairwell turned around in unison, and gave me the same sinister look. Everything around me indicated that I was nanoseconds away from going to Hell. Refusing to accept this reality, I quickly ran back up the staircase and said, "F#@% that! I'm not going there!"

The events I'd witnessed that night transcended time, space, logic, and even state lines. I couldn't deny what I'd seen, nor could I wrap my mind around how an entity, other than God, could orchestrate people like puppets. These elaborate events pointed towards Hell being my future reality, which was tempting to believe. However, later that night, God turned up the volume in my heart and made it clear that not everything I'd seen wasn't from Him, nor did it represent His view of me. This realization came as I sat alone in the car, listening to the radio, and felt a familiar sensation in my chest: what seemed like a second heartbeat with an intellect because it beat perfectly on-time with the music. This feeling encouraged and comforted me, as I remembered that the Bible said that this was God living inside of my heart, and meant that I was His adopted child with an unimaginable inheritance waiting for me in Heaven. But I'm not the only recipient of these gifts...so are you! And soon you'll see how to receive them for yourself!

Piecing Words Together

Anyhow, at this point in my life, despite God's reassurance that I was His child, the attacks on my mind and identity weren't over yet. Another unexpected incident happened one night at work when I came back from break. As I walked through the crowded restaurant, portions of casual remarks from various customers' conversations formed a crystal clear message to me: Upon entering the busy dining room, I heard, "Don't you know." Immediately after that, from an entirely different conversation, I noticed someone say, "That we are." I continued walking between the tables, towards the kitchen, and what stuck out from another group's discussion was, "God and see." Because everything began to feel odd, I stopped for a moment, turned my head, and looked at the person I just heard. I quickly shrugged it off and made my way through the busy restaurant. As I continued back to do my job, my attention was drawn to a part of someone else's remarks, "Everything you're doing." Then, to the left of me, someone said, "And this is why." Just before I reached the entrance to the kitchen, I heard, "You're going to Hell."

I went quickly to the break room to process everything I'd just heard. If you're like me, you might be thinking I'm just crazy: I wondered the same thing myself. However, once again, I experienced something that I couldn't deny but had no idea how it was even possible. Somehow, someway, this message was spoken to me through the mouths of completely random people, timed perfectly, as I walked through the busy restaurant where I worked: "Don't you know that we are God and see everything you're doing? And this is why you're going to Hell."

These experiences robbed me of the sense of reality that I thought I'd regained by moving to Texas. Afterward, while alone, the Holy Spirit inside my heart let me know that He was there and that I was loved and accepted by God, despite the mind-bending encounter I just went through. I had no idea at the time but now know, in retrospect, that this "happening" would be one of the last serious spiritual attacks that I'd ever have in my life. Just as I faced my biggest fears spiritually, I'd soon face what I'd feared most in life: death and the law.

Step Away from the Tracks

A few nights after the strange experience at work, my girlfriend and I got into a huge fight. As I wandered the streets to get away from the drama, Jesus' words kept repeating in my head, from the verse in the Bible which reads, "If your hand makes you stumble, cut it off, and if your eye causes you to stumble, cut it out. For it is better to enter into life with one hand and one eye than to spend eternity in Hell." After everything I'd seen, Hell was an incredibly real place to me, and I wanted no part of it. I heard a train whistle blowing in the distance, and came up with the goofy idea to let the train run over my wrists so I wouldn't have to go to Hell.

I walked up to the tracks, sobbing like a baby, frightened by the thought that I was about to leave this life for good. I told God that I took His Word seriously and begged him to honor what I was about to do. I uncontrollably cried as I thought about my daughter, mother, brothers, and sisters; how this decision would affect them and break their hearts because I'd committed suicide. With tears streaming down my face and snot pouring from my nose, I kneeled next to the tracks, laid my wrists across the rails, and begged God to forgive me. The ground shook violently, and the light coming from the front of the locomotive blinded me. The train approached with great speed, and just before it reached me, I pulled my wrists off the tracks and wept with deep pain because I felt like a coward. As the boxcars roared by, the noise was deafening. I looked up and laughed hysterically as I realized something quite ironic: There were two sets of tracks, and the train was on the set furthest from me. Had I not cowered down and pulled my arms from the rails, I'd still have my life and hands. God saved me from my reckless and self-destructive ways that night, regardless of which choice I'd made.

Time to Face the Music

I wrestled with the voice of my conscience after I left the train tracks that night. It wasn't that I heard two voices in my head, but rather, I had conflicting thoughts in my mind, spoken in the same voice: mine. The conversation began as I thought, "It's time—you need to go to Illinois to turn yourself in. If you don't do it now, you never will." Although I wasn't guilty of the accusations, I reluctantly agreed, because I knew that the only way to deal with the problem was to face it. I got on a bus and headed to Illinois the next day. I fought with my conscience the entire trip. When I got off the bus, I didn't inform my family of what I was doing, but headed straight to the police department and turned myself in.

I learned that I was facing a six-year prison sentence and began to panic because I saw neither hope nor a way to escape this harsh reality. Feeling God inside of my heart was comforting as I sat in my cell, but I still felt very uneasy, because I dreaded the thought of going back to prison. After a week had passed, I talked to an officer about everything that was going on, and they recommended that I move to a different cell block that focused on developing life skills to better the lives of the participants when they got released. I decided to switch cell blocks and discovered afterward that the inmates in the program met regularly to study the Bible, which made doing time a much more positive experience.

First to Go Free

The leader of the group, who did most of the teaching, would often say, "The one who puts his faith in Christ will be the first to go free! Mark my word!" My faith was definitely in Christ, but of everyone on our cellblock, my charges carried the longest sentence. Therefore, I didn't even consider the possibility that I could be the one he was talking about because I was mentally preparing myself for a full-blown prison sentence.

Two weeks after turning myself in, while lying on the bed in my cell, a corrections officer opened my door and said, "Allinger, they want you downstairs for court." When the judge called my case, he said, "Mr. Allinger, the State of Illinois drops all charges against you. You are free to go." I couldn't believe what I'd heard and walked back upstairs in utter amazement. When I got back to the cellblock and told everyone what had happened, the group leader shouted, "See, I told you that the one who put his faith in Christ would be the first to go free!" Had I not listened to the voice of my conscience, doing what I felt God wanted me to do, the charges against me would've never been dropped, and I would've continued to live paranoid and on the run.

Mom's Parallel

After I had been released from jail, my mom informed me that my old best friend's daughter heard that I'd turned myself in and that she went to the police and told them that the allegations against me weren't true. I was very thankful that my name was cleared and for another second chance in life. As my mom and I continued to talk, I told her the story of what happened to me on my birthday at the bar in Texas, before I turned myself in. She responded by telling me that the same thing had happened to her when she was younger, in a stairwell at a bar in Michigan. She described a very similar scenario: she walked down the stairs, and every head turned in unison and looked directly into her eyes. What's different about her story, is that when all the heads turned, their faces shape-shifted into demon-like faces that all gave her evil looks. When everyone turned and looked away from her, their faces shape-shifted back into regular human faces again. I knew that my mom and I had near death experiences in common, but the stairwell story took things to another level which was way more than mere coincidence.

Texas Parallel

Shortly after mom shared her story with me, I had a dream that paralleled what happened to me in Texas before I turned myself in. In the dream, I was at my aunt's house, and a countdown started from 10, 9, 8...on the television screens located throughout her house. I frantically ran around each room, looking for someone to help me. As the countdown hit "2-1," I picked up my phone to call someone to help me, rescue me from going to Hell, but I couldn't think of anyone that was able. When the countdown hit "0," I was staring at my cell phone screen, and then I woke up. I got out of bed, went to the kitchen, picked up my phone and turned it on. When I read the words on the homescreen of my cellphone, the dream made perfect sense, it simply read, "JESUS SAVES."

Time to be a Dad

I spent a few weeks in Illinois, but kept hearing the voice of my conscience say, "You need to go back to Michigan and be a dad." I thought God was directing me back to simply be a father to my daughter. But by making the move, the spiritual attacks that I'd grown used to ceased, and my sense of identity and reality were soon restored. In the years to come, I discovered the new life that God had waiting for me; as I was completely unaware that moving back to be a dad meant that He would give me nine more beautiful, loving children and an adorable grandson.

CHAPTER 6:
REDEEMING THE PRESENT

Surprise, Surprise

I moved back to Michigan, and began living with my biological dad, and attended classes full-time at the Flint Bible Institute and the University of Michigan-Flint, to pursue my Bachelor's Degree in Business Administration. One night in the hallway at school, I ran into my ex-girlfriend; the one in my journal that said I had to marry her to escape 666 and Hell. She'd moved back from Illinois and attended the same college as me. In our conversation, I found out that she had a son and was having relationship problems with his dad. I wanted to tell her that I was interested in dating her again, but was very timid, and didn't have the confidence to say anything in the way of pursuing her.

At the same time, I met a girl at church who I became close friends with because she was fascinated by my stories and didn't think I was crazy. One night at her apartment, I opened up and told her my most shameful secret. Afterward, as I sat there, feeling completely vulnerable and exposed, she looked at me and said, "Wow. I thought that I was the only person who's ever gone through that." Right then, for the first time in years, I felt that someone finally understood me and didn't judge my past.

A few nights and a couple of drinks later, we took it to another level, and things turned romantic. I questioned my intentions for being with her because she wasn't my type at all. Within two weeks, she cheated on me with her ex. After this mishap, her attitude towards me became negative, and we fought constantly. Seeing this part of her personality repelled me so much that I wanted to end things with her altogether. With this in mind, I told her that we needed to talk and she replied, "You're right, we do need to talk. I have something to tell you, too." I asked her to go first, and she said the unexpected, "I'm pregnant. Go ahead, what do you have to say?" With shock in my eyes, I quickly replied, "Never mind. It doesn't matter."

Going into that conversation, I had every intention to cut all ties with her; however, out of my desire to do the right thing, I asked her to marry me. We planned a quick wedding, and as the ceremony approached, our fighting continued to get worse. During one fight, I told her that I didn't want to marry her because I couldn't stand her. I thought that my honesty would make her want to run, but she continued making wedding plans anyway. Deep inside, I wanted to marry my ex and felt that going through with this marriage would be a huge mistake because we weren't in love and didn't even like each other.

Extremely Cold Feet

I called my ex-girlfriend to ask for her advice and she told me, "Just because you have a kid together doesn't mean you have to marry her. Marriage is nothing but a piece of paper anyhow. Just be there for your kids, that's what's most important." I wanted to tell her that she was the one I wanted to marry, but I didn't have the courage. Her advice left me more confused than I already was because we had a fundamentally different view of marriage: she saw marriage simply as a piece of paper, and I saw it more as a lifelong commitment. I felt conflicted, because I had no desire to show up to my wedding, yet I didn't have the heart to leave the mother of my future child standing alone at the altar.

A few nights before the wedding, I told my dad that the only way I was going to get married was if God wanted me to. So, we prayed together, asking God for His direction. The next day, my dad came over to help me move my fiancée's furniture from her apartment into our new place. He asked if I'd received any confirmation yet, but I hadn't. The very second I said this, a series of memories involving the picture that God lit up on the wall played in my mind: First, I remembered the night in my dad's living room when it radiated with a brilliant light which I can barely put into words. Next, I saw the picture again in the memory of watching a DVD of my daughter playing while I lived in Texas; as I remembered this, I realized that it had been filmed in my fiance's' apartment complex. Then, I saw the picture once more in the memory of flipping through the TV channels and randomly landing on the Trinity Broadcasting Network. Finally, I remembered seeing the picture hanging on the wall of a church that my fiance' and I once attended. As all of these memories flashed through my mind, they fit together like puzzle pieces, and it became crystal clear that God wanted me to go through with the marriage. Shortly after our wedding, unbeknownst to everyone in my life, it became very evident that I regretted the decision to follow what I believed God wanted me to do. Although my spiritual attacks had ceased, my dream life became the new battleground for my mind, marriage, and ultimately my identity.

Dreams Affect Reality

A few months into our marriage, I had a dream that I sat in the pew of an empty church, and a minister stood at the pulpit and yelled at me in a language I didn't understand. I stood up and angrily yelled back at him but had no idea what I said, because I spoke a foreign language, too. Suddenly, the voice of God spoke in a different unknown language, causing downward waves of distortion in the blue projection screens on the sides of the pulpit, as it came down from above. When I heard His voice, I prayed for the ability to translate what He said, but I didn't understand a word. After He stopped talking, five nails the size of baseball bats flew from behind the stage; one nail abruptly carried the minister out of the church by his suit coat, and the other nails securely pinned the two massive, arched wooden doors of the sanctuary wide-open.

A man standing on the right-hand side of the stage chuckled, then sarcastically said, "Well, it looks like he was wrong!" In a confused tone, I replied, "I guess so." We walked into a room and stood face-to-face at a tall table. For some reason, I explained to Him how the Holy Spirit lives in our hearts and how it takes a little time to get used to. He replied, "You're right, it's taken me some time to get used to it myself." And asked the question, "Amos, what would you say if I showed you this?" Then he held out his hand and in it was a set of copper scales balanced on an arrow. One side of the scale had a tarnished penny infused into it, the other side was empty, and between the scales was a little opened hand that protruded off to the side. Then, I saw a shiny new penny lying on the floor, which prompted me to reply, "A measure of wheat for a penny, and three measures of barley for a penny; and see you hurt not the oil and the wine." Suddenly, the copper hand closed, opened back up, and written on its palm was the word "OH."

This dream had no significance until I read Revelation 6:5, which says, "...he that sat on him had a pair of scales in his hand." Then, I read my exact response to His question, word-for-word in Revelation 6:6, and realized that this is the 6th verse, of the 6th chapter, in the 66th book of the Bible. I knew that God was trying to tell me something and that it couldn't be a coincidence that I had this dream; especially considering the mental torment that I'd experienced for years, due to what I wrote in my journal about needing to marry my ex to escape the sixes and Hell.

It was impossible to commit myself to my wife because I felt that my marriage was a mistake. I mistakenly believed that cheating on her was the quickest and easiest way out, which lead me to break my vows. I waited to confess my mistake until after our son was born, knowing that it was a heartless act that a pregnant woman shouldn't have to shoulder. I expected her to leave me, but she forgave me instead. This hit me completely off-guard, and her willingness to forgive so quickly felt like love, which made me lose sight of why I'd tried to leave in the first place. Shortly after our reconciliation, we found out that my wife was pregnant with our second child.

There's No Goodbye

I began building our new house and halfway through the project, my step dad stopped by to join me for lunch and had an in-depth conversation about what was happening in his life. Little did I know that this would be the last time I would see his face. Two weeks before my newest daughter was born, I received a phone call informing me that my stepdad had been hit by a drunk driver and died in a car accident. For the next several months I was severely depressed and could barely do anything because all the hurtful things I'd ever said to him while he was alive continually replayed in my mind.

After not working on the house for two months, I forced myself to finish building it to take my mind off everything. When I completed its construction, my struggle with the journal and the sixes reared its ugly head. It seemed that no matter what I did, I couldn't get over what I'd written, and it seemed nearly impossible to change. To rid myself of it once and for all, I prayed and asked God for a second son as a sign that I could finally let it go and move on with my life. Within weeks, my wife was pregnant with our third child. I was so excited and felt that God had quickly answered my prayer; that is until we found out that we were having another girl. I wasn't disappointed at all to have a third daughter, but I felt like God was directing me back towards my ex. I felt like a lunatic who was completely lost and unable to get closure from the past.

No Son, No Thank You

Our daughter was born at a hospital near my hometown of Fisher, Illinois. While there, I came up with a simple plan to rid myself of the sixes on my Michigan license by getting my original license back from Illinois, which had zero sixes on it. For the first time in years, I had a sense of mental freedom and felt that I'd finally defeated the ridiculousness that had haunted me for too many years. The victory was short-lived and only lasted for a few months: The vicious cycle started all over again, and I convinced myself that I had to either have a second son or marry my ex, to escape the mental prison I'd put myself in. So, I asked God once again to give me another sign, that if we had a boy, it meant I could let my journal entry go and if our baby was a girl, I was supposed to leave my wife and be with my ex. Shortly afterward, we found out that she was pregnant with our fourth child. Three months later, an ultrasound revealed that we were having another girl. I instantly became distant toward my wife and prepared myself to leave her for good.

The Girl of My Dreams

One day at work, I ran into the mother of a girl who I found very attractive, and she told me that her daughter had a seizure the night before. I felt compassion towards her daughter and a sense of familiarity because I'd dealt with my mom's seizures a few times in the past. After hearing about her seizure, I felt drawn to her more than I ever had before. A month before my fourth daughter was born, the girl and her older sister began working as my secretaries. She was one of the most beautiful girls I'd ever seen. She had amazing blue eyes, a gorgeous smile, and was so pretty that she didn't even need to wear makeup. I didn't cheat on my wife, but I honestly wanted to.

While at the hospital, awaiting the birth of my fourth daughter, I remembered a dream that I'd had about my new secretary and crush, years before we'd ever met. In the dream, I walked up to a man who said, "Welcome to the eternal incubator." Then, I was walking around inside an enormous circus tent, ran into the girl, and asked, "Are you the one?" With no response, she led me to a room, which I entered alone. I found myself in complete darkness, with my entire body covered in flames that I could only feel, not see. In a panic, I repeatedly sang at the top of my lungs, "Holy, Holy, Holy, is the Lord God Almighty!" Somehow, singing kept the fire from hurting me. Suddenly, I was back in the hallway walking toward the girl, and she whispered in my ear, "Why didn't you tell me more about yourself?"

After I had realized that my secretary was the girl in my dreams, I felt drawn to her even more than I already was. My wife and I separated, and I moved into my own apartment. Soon afterward, my secretary and I began dating. I kept our relationship secret and off social media because I wasn't divorced, which caused a lot of problems and break-ups in my new relationship. One time, we got back together and found out she was pregnant. Our past breakups made me doubt if I was the father.

Fooling Myself

Overtaken by the thought of leaving my kids to be with someone potentially pregnant with another man's child, I lost sight of why I even left my wife in the first place. My wife and I got back together, and our reconciliation required me to ignore my pregnant ex. We fought a lot about my infidelity, and things got much worse once the baby was born, especially when we realized that my old secretary's baby was mine. She gave birth to my fifth daughter, who looked just like me. I wasn't allowed to see her, but I did sneak to visit her once. To be honest, I didn't know how to handle the situation at all.

When my youngest daughter was four months old, her mother texted me and asked if I was ever going to be a part of our child's life. I met up with her and my daughter that day and was drawn to my ex once again, which made me realize that I wanted to be with her instead of my wife. One day, while sitting in the car together, I asked that she put her hand on my chest as we listened to classical music on the radio. I prayed for God to allow her to feel Him inside my heart, and if she did, that it would mean this was the woman He wanted me to be with. I didn't tell her that I prayed this, but when I asked her if she could feel it, she said she did. I'd asked my ex-wife to do this before in the past, but she never felt anything and just looked at me like I was crazy. The fact that my youngest daughter's mother felt the Holy Spirit was proof to me that I made the right decision, as hard as it was to go through. We prayed that if God wanted us to be together, He would give us another child. Three weeks later, she took a pregnancy test, and it was positive.

So Forgetful

Within a few weeks, we discovered that she was going to have a boy.. I felt like I was on the verge of freedom, because I'd have my second son, and could finally put the lunacy of the sixes and my journal behind me...or so I'd thought. Just shy of a year after he was born, we found out that she was pregnant again with my third son and eighth child. The summer after he was born, we finally got married. A few months later, we got into a big fight, and somehow I'd forgot the answer that I'd received from God and started to struggle with what I'd written in my journal. I questioned whether I'd married the right person again, so we decided to take a break from our marriage, which allowed me to put closure on what I'd written about my past.

Sixes No More

After contacting the ex I'd write about in my journal and telling her that she was the only one who could help me defeat the devil, I realized how incredibly insane it was for me to allow what I'd written all those years ago to have so much control over my life. I humbly remembered that God had already given me a second son as a sign to say that I could finally let the 666 thing go. It became crystal clear to me that my salvation had nothing to do with my journal and had everything to do with Christ dying on the cross for me. Feeling the Spirit in my heart is all the proof I'll ever need that I have a place waiting for me in Heaven. I realized that the Holy Spirit had been knocking on my heart the whole time that I was going through these trials. All along God was screaming, in an ever-so-soft whisper, "You're Mine, you belong to Me, Heaven is yours; there's no need for you to prove your salvation any other way. What you wrote in your journal doesn't matter. What's important is that I am inside of you, letting you know that I am here and that you are Mine." I've always said, "To know me and to stay, is to love me." This is how I know God loves me: He's been there through every foolish decision and has seen every thought I've ever had, yet He's still here inside my heart. This revelation has completely liberated me from the mistakes of my past and has solidified who I really am: I am a child of God; forgiven, sealed, loved, adored, and saved from the repercussions of my many foolish decisions that had brought me to this point. But guess what? I'm not the only one! So are you!

Sorry for the Pain

Putting my kids and family through all the pain of my quest for salvation, was one of the hardest things I've ever dealt with in my life. I was still in love with my new wife and wanted our marriage to work. Thankfully, she understood my crazy logic, forgave me, and we got back together. She gave birth to our third son and fourth child, my fourth son and ninth child, nine months later. Within two months of our son's birth, I finished the rough draft of this book, and my oldest daughter gave birth to my first grandchild, a beautiful baby boy. My friend and mentor got involved with the book to help me get it edited and published. Working with him made me realize that my book was nothing more than a journal and was far from completion. A year after working on it with him, we were getting ready to publish, and I found out that my wife was pregnant with my fifth son.

The Kids Need Me

After my wife, kids, and I had celebrated my mom's birthday with her, we got home, and I had a massive heart attack which nearly killed me. While in the hospital before surgery to remove the blockage in my heart, all I could think was that I wasn't ready to die, because my kids needed me. It was a sobering experience that put things into perspective and made me appreciate everyday life, my wife, and all the kids so much more.

Living the Life

Earlier this year, before my tenth child was born, my ex-wife and her new husband got criminal charges pressed against them for hitting two of my kids, which resulted in me filing for custody. What I've learned during the custody battle is something that I didn't understand before: that God views us the way I view my kids and loves us more deeply than any of us love our children. I adore my kids and there's nothing they could ever do that would make me turn my back on them or change my love for them. We are God's children, and this is how He feels about us. I would do anything for my kids to show them that I love them and to protect them. Likewise, God shows us that He loved us by becoming a man, Jesus, and to protect us from the forces of darkness and the consequences of sin, He died for us. Without Him dying on the cross, we wouldn't be able to experience God inside of our hearts; this is one of the most important things His sacrifice purchased. And in so doing, He made us His children, and the Spirit living in our hearts is proof. As a parent, if I had to die on a cross to protect my kids, to take their place for something wrong they'd done, or to simply show them that I love them more than anything else in this world, I would. We see what Christ suffered on the cross, and dare

69

I say that it was nothing for Him. As brutal as it was, if He had to do it all over again, He would. Why? Because He loves us. And more particularly, He loves you.

So, now that you've read my story, you may wonder why I've given all of the details of my life. My hopes are that you'll see that you don't have to go through this life alone, and that your past mistakes aren't uncommon. If you feel guilt, shame, regret, or any other negative emotions toward your past, please don't. Making mistakes is part of being a human and, if you share your story, God can use your mistakes to help other people get through their struggles in life, by turning your mess into a message. Through sharing your pain and being vulnerable, you can find liberty, healing, and purpose.

In the next chapter, I'll show you some of the evidence in God's Word that validates the Truth that you can find Him living inside of your heart. Prepare yourself to come to this understanding: When you finally feel God in your heart, if you haven't already, it means you are His child, and that He loves you unconditionally. It also means that you have an unimaginable inheritance waiting for you, not only now, but when you leave this life, as well. Additionally, it means that you'll live forever! You'll have the seal of God upon you, proof that you are His forever and He is yours forever, and that no one can ever take Him from you. You'll have your own portion of the Truth that you can take with you anywhere in this world and never be alone again. Soon, you'll experience God in a way that will change the rest of your entire life for the better, as you'll be one of the first in our generation to experience "God's Next Evolutionary Steps For Mankind!"

✿
CHAPTER 7:
THE SUPPORTING EVIDENCE

Before you ask God to give you this gift, the question is: What evidence is there, besides experiencing it for yourself, that this is the Truth? And is this evident in the Word of God? Absolutely! What I'm talking about is not something that I've made up, but rather a reality that exists for all believers. Because there are so many verses on this topic, I've hand-picked the ones that touch on each subcategory that I think say it best and have italicized the parts that support each heading. Rather than me interpreting these for you, I'd like you to read the following verses and allow the Word of God to speak for itself.

The reality that God lives in us:

2 Timothy 1:13-14 - "Take as your norm the sound words that you heard from me, in the faith and love that are in Christ Jesus. Guard this rich trust with the help of *the Holy Spirit that dwells within us.*"

1 Corinthians 3:16 -"Do you not know that *you are the temple of God*, and that the *Spirit of God dwells in you?*"

Psalm 46:11 - "*Be still and know that I am God.* I am exalted among the nations, exalted on the earth."

God can be found living inside our actual hearts:

Romans 5:4-6 - "And hope does not disappoint *because the love of God has been poured out into our hearts through the Holy Spirit that has been given to us.* For Christ, while we were still helpless, yet died at the appointed time for the ungodly."

2 Peter 1:19 - "Moreover, we possess the prophetic message that is altogether reliable. You will do well to be attentive to it, as to a lamp shining in a dark place, *until day dawns and the morning star rises in your hearts.*"

Galatians 4:6 - "*As proof that you are children, God sent the spirit of his Son into our hearts,* crying out, "Abba, Father!"

We are God's children:

John 14:16-18 - "And I will ask the Father, and he will give you another Advocate to be with you always, the Spirit of truth, which the world cannot accept because it neither sees nor knows it. But you know it, because it remains with you, *and will be in you. I will not leave you orphans; I will come to you.*"

Romans 8:15-16 - "For you did not receive a spirit of slavery to fall back into fear, but *you received a spirit of adoption*, through which we cry, "Abba, Father!" The *Spirit itself bears witness with our spirit that we are children of God.*"

John 3:7 - "Do not be amazed that I told you, *'You must be born from above.'*"

1 John 5:1-3 - "*Everyone who believes that Jesus is the Christ is* *begotten by God,* and everyone who loves the Father loves the one begotten by Him."

Titus 3:4-6 - "But when the kindness and generous love of God our savior appeared, not because of any righteous deeds we had done but because of his mercy, he saved us *through the bath of rebirth and renewal by the Holy Spirit, whom he richly poured out on us* through Jesus Christ, our Savior."

The Holy Spirit is the proof of our inheritance:

Ephesians 1:13-14 - "In him you also, who have heard the word of truth, the gospel of your salvation, and have believed in him, *were sealed with the promised Holy Spirit, which is the first installment of our inheritance toward redemption as God's possession,* to the praise of his glory."

2 Corinthians 1:21-23 - "But the one who gives us security with you in Christ and who anointed us is God; *he has also put his seal upon us and given the Spirit in our hearts as a first installment.*"

How we receive this amazing gift:

John 7:38-39 - "Whoever believes in me, as scripture says: '*Rivers of living water will flow from within him.*'" He said this in reference to *the Spirit that those who came to believe in him were to receive...*"

Acts 2:38 - "Peter [said] to them, '*Repent and be baptized, every one of you, in the name of Jesus Christ for the forgiveness of your sins;* and you will receive the gift of the Holy Spirit.*'"

Luke 11:9-13- "And I tell you, ask and you will receive; seek and you will find; knock and the door will be opened to you. For everyone who asks, receives; and the one who seeks, finds; and to the one who knocks, the door will be opened. What father among you would hand his son a snake when he asks for a fish? Or hand him a scorpion when he asks for an egg? If you then, who are wicked, know how to give good gifts to your children, *how much more will the Father in heaven give the Holy Spirit to those who ask Him?*"

❋
CHAPTER 8:
TAKE THE LEAP!

If you haven't believed in God in the past, all you must do to find out that He exists is do what my little brother did when he was an atheist and opened himself up to the possibility that God is real. He said a "prayer" that went something like this: "God, if you're real, please reveal Yourself to me and prove that You exist." That's all he "prayed." God was faithful and answered his prayer. However, when he prayed, it was towards the sky, hoping that God had heard Him. Rather than praying towards the sky, I'd like you to pray inwardly, in your mind, but towards your heart, because that is where you'll find God. Pray this prayer: "God, if you exist, please reveal Yourself to me. If what I'm reading is the Truth, and Your Word is True, I believe that Jesus is the Christ and invite the Holy Spirit to live in my heart and start communicating with me."

If you've prayed this prayer, congratulations, you're about to have an incredible lifelong experience and have just become a child of God! In the future, and for the rest of your life, you'll find your connection and interaction with God by simply focusing on your heartbeat, and noticing that the Spirit responds to anything you listen to, watch, or say inside your mind. When you talk to God, it won't be a question of whether He hears you or not, because you'll KNOW He does. What your mind needs to experience is that God sees and hears all your thoughts. Yes, it may seem a little creepy or scary at first, but don't worry, over time you'll learn that God loves you unconditionally.

If you've "prayed" for God to prove His existence, or if you're already a believer, this is the point in the book that I'd like you to practice feeling God in your heart. The first thing you'll need to do is pay attention to the feeling of your heartbeat. It may seem a little unfamiliar and uncomfortable when you do this, but over time, it will become second nature. You'll should start to feel everything you pay attention to in your mind start to "beat" in your heart. At first, this will require quite a bit of concentration, so I suggest that you go into a room by yourself and get the distractions down to a minimum. Turn on some music that you enjoy and close your eyes so that you can focus on your heart and hone in on one voice or instrument. If you prefer silence, you can keep your eyes open and watch a flickering flame or blinking light, while at the same time, focusing in on your heartbeat. Soon, you'll notice that the sights or sounds that you pay attention to feel as though they're originating from inside of your heart. What you're feeling is the Holy Spirit of God, who is God Himself. You'll come to understand that the Holy Spirit is on cue with everything you pay attention to, and learn that He knows every word and every note of every song. As you experiment with this phenomenon two verses in the Bible will begin to make perfect sense:

Psalm 46:10 - *"Be still and KNOW that I AM God"*

and

John 16:13 - "But when He comes, the Spirit of Truth, He will guide you to all Truth. *He will not speak on His own, but He will speak what He hears,* and will declare to you the things that are coming."

The first verse teaches that to KNOW that God exists, all you have to do is be still...because He is in you and the only way to truly turn your focus inward is by doing just that: being still. The second verse teaches us that the Holy Spirit speaks what he hears. This is a bit of a mystery but my experience with the Holy Spirit has taught me that I never really hear Him speak, per say, but I He does "beat" everything that I hear inside of my heart. This shows me that He hears my thoughts and that He speaks to us personally without using any words. I suppose it would be similar to being married to someone who couldn't speak...they have the ability to show you that you are loved without saying a word' they would show you their love and affectionately display their love for you likely by touch. This is how I know you can experience God, too.

To help you understand the reality that God lives inside of you, I relate the experience to a baby living inside and kicking its mother's belly whenever it wishes. A baby does not intentionally kick its mother, and it seems to happen at the most random and inconvenient of times. When a woman is pregnant, she's fully aware of the life inside of her, because of its movements, kicks, hiccups, and such. Similarly, whether you're a male or female, you have the ability to be "pregnant" in your heart with a living being that is as innocent as a baby. The only difference is that the gentle "kicks" that you'll feel inside are intentional, and the Spirit will experientially show you that He has an intellect and the ability to understand and interact with your every thought. It is when you make this discovery, that you'll see God is directly communicating with you. Just as the Virgin Mary had Deity living inside of her, you'll have Deity living inside of you. The only difference is that that Deity will never leave your body and is there to stay. In this process, your mind and heart will begin an ongoing communication that will last for the rest of your life.

What you'll feel inside your heart is akin this: grip one of your fingers with your hand and listen to something, then squeeze your hand in sync with whatever you're paying attention to. Squeeze every word that you hear on the radio or something you see on television with a gentle squeeze. The feeling you sense on the finger you're gripping will be like what you'll feel in your heart. However, it won't be your hand squeezing your heart; it will be the Hand of God.

First, realize that this gift of love inside your heart has been purchased with a price; it cost the Son of God His life. His sacrifice afforded you this personal relationship and experience with God. Know that the Holy Spirit can never be taken away from you and that you'll never be alone, because God will be right inside of you. This Spiritual exercise will let you know that He's with you every single step of the way. You'll never have to feel alone again or question whether God loves or forgives you...He does! And He's right there inside your heart to prove it.

Remember that the Holy Spirit who lives inside of you is called the Counselor. He is there for you to talk with about anything you want. He desires more than anything to become your closest friend and confidant. Begin praying or talking to Him inwardly, in your mind, and feel Him beat the words of your conversation in your heart. It is a phenomenal and eye-opening experience, understanding that God is there with you, in your heart, reading your mind...and that He loves you, accepts you, and forgives you, regardless. At this point in the book, I'd like you to stop reading, put the book down, and experiment with feeling God interact with you inside your heart. Until you feel Him for yourself, please don't read any further. I'll give you some steps on what to do next when you come back. For now, just spend some time getting to know the loving Hand of God.

✿
CONCLUSION:
WHAT'S NEXT?

So, what about the devil? Do I want you to know that he is real and interact with him? Not really. I've shared all the details of my testimony with the hope that you could see that just as God is real, so is His enemy. The devil has an evil agenda against the children of God, which means that we are unknowingly in a battle with Dad's enemy. Per the Word of God, we have an active role to play in defeating the devil. The book of Revelation 12:1 reads, "They conquered him [the devil] by the blood of the Lamb and by the word of their testimony; love for life did not deter them from death."

The blood of the Lamb had already been shed when Jesus died for us on the cross. However, the second part of the equation has not taken place yet. This is where you and I have an active role to play in conquering the devil in our lives and families: "They [We] conquered him [the devil] ...by the word of their testimony." This book, my brothers and sisters, is my testimony, but it is not sufficient to conquer the enemy because it says THEY CONQUERED HIM. I take this to mean that the children of God (Us) come together and share their testimonies, and in so doing, conquer the devil. Therefore, I encourage all of you, children of God, who read this book or hear this message to share your testimonies...which simply means stories...so sharing our stories with each other is highly imperative!

God can turn your mess into a message that can touch the hearts and lives of many people if you open yourself up and allow it to happen. Sharing your story is liberating, and it can help you find freedom from your past and purpose for your life. If you're new to the faith or have been a believer for years, and you've started feeling God within your heart, I encourage you to share your experience and stories. You may be wondering about what you do next, and I refuse to leave you hanging without giving you some sort of game plan.

If you are a new believer, I strongly suggest you do the following:

Begin reading the Word of God, starting in the New Testament, at the Book of John (it's after the book of Luke but before the book of Acts) and read it repeatedly until it Becomes part of your memory. At that point, read the next book following John and read it as many times as it takes until it begins to sink in. The Gospel of John really puts the love of God into perspective and the life of Jesus. It is His story and it's true. So when you read it try keeping the perspective that it IS HIS-TORY. You'll notice a lot of verses that talk about the Spirit that lives in you and your being a child of God. To me, the Gospel of John is the best book in the Bible. Then the book of Acts is all about the Holy Spirit when He came to the first believers after Jesus came back from the dead and returned to Heaven. That's why this is my second favorite book in the Bible: it's all about the Holy Spirit!

Get in the habit of thanking God every day for all the blessings in your life. Do your best to fulfill the great commandment given to us by Christ; Love God and Love people. He tells us that we are to forgive and not judge. People are going through painful situations that you have no idea about. Treating them with love, respect, and compassion will come back to you in the long run. Find a good, Bible-based church or group of believers that you can start fellowshipping with on a regular basis. Doing so will help to build your faith, answer your questions, and utilize your talents in helping serve the Kingdom of God. But be warned: there are many different sects of believers and lots of confusion out there. Before getting involved with any one group, study the Word of God for yourself, and allow the Spirit of Truth to teach you. Common false teachings to be aware of include, but are not limited to, the following:

• Teaching that claims you can earn or do good to receive your salvation.

• Focusing on the demonic activity and/or blaming the devil for everything bad.

• Sinning with other believers because of the freedom given to God's children.

• Giving money to receive miracles from God or His forgiveness.

• Teaching that says speaking in tongues is the only proof of having God's Spirit.

God's gifts of the Holy Spirit and salvation cost you absolutely nothing! It cost Jesus His life, and that's all it will ever require. If you feel the Spirit in your heart, that's all the proof you'll ever need that God lives inside you. If anyone teaches you that you can buy the Holy Spirit, salvation, or miracles, walk away and never return to that place. Yes, as children of God, we are completely forgiven for all our sins but do not use that freedom to do what you know is wrong. We are supposed to be imitators of God, doing our best to resist sin and love everyone we encounter. We are called to forgive one another and not judge others.

EPILOGUE:
LEARN AND SHARE

There's so much more that I could teach about what it means to be a believer and the next steps to take in your walk of faith with God, but I do not want to complicate the message of this book. So I've made the free app "OMG It's True!" available on the App Store if you want to learn more about the next steps to take in your walk with God.

More than my desire to defeat the enemy is my desire to touch the hearts and lives of the people in the world. With these motivators in mind, I've created a Facebook group called "OMG It's True! Your Stories!" This group was created for people to share their stories of how God has worked in their lives and how they, too, have experienced the Hand of God inside of their hearts. If you'd like to share your story or would like to read the testimonies of others, please join the group "OMG IT'S TRUE! Your Stories!" on Facebook. I've also created a fan page on Facebook called "OMG It's True! By Amos Allinger" that will share what people are saying about their experiences with the Hand of God inside of their hearts, as well. My hope is to grow a community of believers who share their experiences with God; to help build the faith of other believers and those curious to see what the Hand of God is doing in the lives of other people.

For now, my work here is done. In this book, I've shared with you the Truth that God will come to live inside of your heart, by simply asking Him, and that He's ready to have a One-on-one interaction with you there, which will last every day for the rest of your life. I've given you examples of how to feel Him inside of yourself, by focusing on your thoughts and your Heartbeat at the same time. I've shown you the Scriptural evidence that He lives inside of us and what it means; namely, that God loves you, forgives you, accepts you, sees you as His child, and has sent His Spirit into your heart as a guarantee that you have an inheritance available now and when you leave this life...and live forever!

If this book has touched you in any way and you think that it could help someone in need, please send them to the website **www.omgitstrue.com** to download a free copy of this book to their computers, tablets, or smartphones! Thank you for reading this book. It was truly my pleasure and honor to bring it to you. God bless you!!! Amos